BIZARRE CRIMES

by DON DOUGHERTY

DODD, MEAD & COMPANY, NEW YORK

Printed in the United States of America

1 2 3 4 5 6 7 8 9 10

Library of Congress Catalog Card Number: 81-67790
ISBN: 0-396-08010-3

A MASTERMIND OF MISCHIEF IS ON THE LOOSE.
BIZARRE CRIMES ARE PERPETRATED BY A DIABOLICAL GENIUS WHO IS ENDOWED WITH A RATHER SILLY SENSE OF CRIME. WHERE WILL HE STRIKE? WHAT WILL HE DO? WHO WILL BE NEXT?
PRECINCT 13
WANTED
BIZARRE CRIMES FILE VOL. 32

SANITATION

POST NO BILLS
BILL
STAPLES

SUPER GLUE

VANILL
CHOCOLAT
NUTS

HELIUM

STOP ME
BEFORE I
COAL
MORE!

SPAGHETTI

702
701
CHARMIN
CHARMIN

VICTOR'S
SEAFOOD
RESTAURANT

LIVER
WURST

ORTHOPEDIC CLINIC
ORTHOPEDICS
DR. J.P. SNIPE

7
13
25
91

JUMBO SIZE
BAND AIDS

DDS
DENTAL
CLINIC

PEANUT
BUTTER
CHUNKY

AUDUBON
BIRD
GUIDE

TAPIOCA

TO BE CONTINUED...
CIRCUS DAY SALE
BUS
RINGADING BROS. CIRCUS